AR Level: 4.7

Pts. 1.0

Lexile: 720L

Text
STYLES

# HOW TO WRITE A
# FANTASY
## STORY

 Crabtree Publishing Company

www.crabtreebooks.com

Text STYLES

**Author:** Natalie Hyde

**Publishing plan research
and series development:** Reagan Miller

**Editor:** Anastasia Suen

**Proofreader:** Wendy Scavuzzo

**Logo design:** Samantha Crabtree

**Print coordinator:** Katherine Berti

**Production coordinator:** Margaret Amy Salter

**Prepress technicians:** Margaret Amy Salter, Katherine Berti

**Photographs**:

Alamy: foto-zone: pages 6 (top), 24 (bottom);
C. and M. History Pictures: pages 17 (top),
24 (center right)
Bridgeman Art Library: Barry, Jonathan: pages 8 and 15
(top right)
Shutterstock: Neftali: pages 6 (bottom), 15 (bottom left
and right)
Superstock: Walt Disney Productions: pages 18, 19;
Buyenlarge: page 22
All other images by Shutterstock

**Library and Archives Canada Cataloguing in Publication**

Hyde, Natalie, 1963-, author
    How to write a fantasy story / Natalie Hyde.

(Text styles)
Includes index.
Issued in print and electronic formats.
ISBN 978-0-7787-1654-9 (bound).--ISBN 978-0-7787-1659-4 (pbk.).--
ISBN 978-1-4271-9864-8 (pdf).--ISBN 978-1-4271-9869-3 (html)

    1. Fantasy fiction--Authorship--Juvenile literature.  I. Title.
II. Series: Text styles

PN3377.5.F34H93 2014     j808.3'8766     C2014-903772-4
                                     C2014-903773-2

**Library of Congress Cataloging-in-Publication Data**

Hyde, Natalie, 1963- author.
  How to write a fantasy story / Natalie Hyde.
    pages cm. -- (Text styles)
  Includes index.
  ISBN 978-0-7787-1654-9 (reinforced library binding) --
  ISBN 978-0-7787-1659-4 (pbk.) --
  ISBN 978-1-4271-9864-8 (electronic pdf) --
  ISBN 978-1-4271-9869-3 (electronic html)
  1. Fantasy fiction--Authorship--Juvenile literature.  I. Title.

  PN3377.5.F34H93 2014
  808.3'8766--dc23

                      2014022775

# Crabtree Publishing Company

www.crabtreebooks.com     1-800-387-7650                                 Printed in Hong Kong/082014/BK2014061

**Published in Canada
Crabtree Publishing**
616 Welland Ave.
St. Catharines, Ontario
L2M 5V6

**Published in the United States
Crabtree Publishing**
PMB 59051
350 Fifth Avenue, 59th Floor
New York, New York 10118

**Published in the United Kingdom
Crabtree Publishing**
Maritime House
Basin Road North, Hove
BN41 1WR

**Published in Australia
Crabtree Publishing**
3 Charles Street
Coburg North
VIC 3058

# Contents

# What Is a Fantasy Story?

Imagine a world in which wizards, mermaids, trolls, dragons, and faeries live. Where time travel, mind reading, and magic are common. This is the world of fantasy stories. Fantasy stories come straight from our imaginations. They center on events that could not take place in the natural world. Sometimes they are set in a different world, separate from ours. Other times, they take place in a hidden side of our world.

Every culture has stories that are very old. They often have fantasy details in them. Ancient Greek stories had magic, gods, and monsters. Stories from ancient Japan have dragons and magic swords.

 **Fantasy stories are an escape from the real world.**

There are two types of fantasy stories. They are low fantasy and high fantasy. Low fantasy stories usually take place in the real world. They only have a few magical **elements**. Toys might come to life, or animals might talk to humans. *Stuart Little* and *The Borrowers* are low fantasy.

High fantasy stories are different. They take place in completely made-up worlds. These worlds have their own rules and creatures. *The Chronicles of Narnia* and Tolkien's *The Hobbit* are examples of high fantasy.

# Prose, Poetry, or Drama?

Stories can be written down in different ways. In literature, we use different names to talk about the way words are used. The example below shows the same part of a story called *The Lion, the Witch and the Wardrobe*, written in three different ways: as **prose**, a **poem**, and a **drama**.

## Poetry

The Faun was surprised and gave a shout.
He dropped his parcels all about.

"Good gracious me!" he quickly cried.
"Good evening, good evening," Lucy replied.

He said, "Let me gather my things just now,"
And then he gave her a little bow.

## Prose

He was a Faun. And when he saw Lucy he gave such a start of surprise that he dropped all his parcels.

"Goodness gracious me!" exclaimed the Faun.

"Good evening," said Lucy. But the Faun was so busy picking up its parcels that at first it did not reply. When it had finished it made her a little bow.

by C.S. Lewis

## Drama

TIME: Early afternoon in winter

PLACE: On a path in the woods of Narnia

[MR TUMNUS, *the faun, is coming through the woods carrying parcels. He meets* LUCY *who has just come through the wardrobe.*]

[MR TUMNUS *jumps in the surprise and drops all his parcels.*]

MR TUMNUS: Good gracious me!

LUCY: Good evening.

To tell a story in prose, we use sentences. To tell a story with a poem, we use short phrases or groups of words.

When a story is performed as a play, it is called a drama. Can you see the stage directions? They let the actors know when and where things happen.

# The Lion, the Witch and the Wardrobe

*The Lion, the Witch and the Wardrobe* is an example of high fantasy. It is the story of four children; Lucy, Peter, Edmund, and Susan Pevensie. They are sent to a country home in England. They are trying to escape the bombing of the Second World War. They are sent to Professor Digory Kirke's house.

Lucy is the first to discover a magic **wardrobe** in the house. It leads to the magic land of Narnia. It is ruled by the evil White Witch.

## Chapters 1 and 2

*In about ten minutes she reached it and found that it was a lamp-post. As she stood looking at it, wondering why there was a lamp-post in the middle of a wood and wondering what to do next, she heard a pitter patter of feet coming towards her. And soon after that a very strange person stepped out from among the trees into the light of the lamp-post.*

*He was only a little taller than Lucy herself and he carried over his head an umbrella, white with snow. From the waist upwards he was like a man, but his legs were shaped like a goat's (the hair on them was glossy black) and instead of feet he had goat's hoofs. He also had a tail, but Lucy did not notice this at first because it was neatly caught up over the arm that held the umbrella so as to keep it from trailing in the snow. He had a red woollen muffler round his neck and his skin was rather reddish too. He had a strange, but pleasant little face, with a short pointed beard and curly hair, and out of the hair there stuck two horns, one on each side of his forehead. One of his hands, as I have said, held the umbrella: in the other arm he carried several brown-paper parcels.*

What with the parcels and the snow it looked just as if he had been doing his Christmas shopping. He was a Faun. And when he saw Lucy he gave such a start of surprise that he dropped all his parcels.

"Goodness gracious me!" exclaimed the Faun.

"Good evening," said Lucy. But the Faun was so busy picking up its parcels that at first it did not reply. When it had finished it made her a little bow.

"Good evening, good evening," said the Faun. "Excuse me—I don't want to be inquisitive—but should I be right in thinking that you are a Daughter of Eve?"

"My name's Lucy," said she, not quite understanding him.

"But you are—forgive me—you are what they call a girl?" asked the Faun.

"Of course I'm a girl," said Lucy.

"You are in fact Human?"

"Of course I'm human," said Lucy, still a little puzzled.

"To be sure, to be sure," said the Faun. "How stupid of me! But I've never seen a Son of Adam or a Daughter of Eve before. I am delighted. That is to say—" and then it stopped as if it had been going to say something it had not intended but had remembered in time. "Delighted, delighted," it went on. "Allow me to introduce myself. My name is Tumnus."

"I am very pleased to meet you, Mr Tumnus," said Lucy.

"And may I ask, O Lucy Daughter of Eve," said Mr Tumnus, "how you have come into Narnia?"

"Narnia? What's that?" said Lucy.

"This is the land of Narnia," said the Faun, "where we are now; all that lies between the lamp-post and the great castle of Cair Paravel on the eastern sea. And you—you have come from the wild woods of the west?"

"I—I got in through the wardrobe in the spare room," said Lucy.

"Ah!" said Mr Tumnus in a rather melancholy voice, "if only I had worked harder at geography when I was a little Faun, I should no doubt know all about those strange countries. It is too late now."

"But they aren't countries at all," said Lucy, almost laughing. "It's only just back there—at least—I'm not sure. It is summer there."

"Meanwhile," said Mr Tumnus, "it is winter in Narnia, and has been for ever so long, and we shall both catch cold if we stand here talking in the snow. Daughter of Eve from the far land of Spare Oom where eternal summer reigns around the bright city of War Drobe, how would it be if you came and had tea with me?"

# Fantasy Elements

What types of things are found in fantasy stories? Almost anything you can imagine! Fantasy stories have no limits as to what can happen. Mirrors can be gateways to other worlds. In those worlds, flutes can sing, dragons can be pets, a ring can have incredible power, or people can fly.

Magic is a common element in fantasy stories. Spells and curses are made and broken. Objects can have powers, too. In *Harry Potter*, paintings on the wall could talk and the staircases moved on their own.

Supernatural **powers** are also found in fantasy books. People can read minds, see ghosts, or see the future. Superheroes often have special skills to make them unique. Superman could see through walls and lift trains.

Fantasy elements allow the characters to have new experiences that would not be possible in the real world. They create excitement and suspense in the story.

Mythical **creatures** are also found in these stories. Unicorns, dragons, trolls, and pixies are just some of the creatures that can exist in a fantasy world. In *The Lion, the Witch and the Wardrobe*, Lucy meets a faun. A faun is half goat and half human. Fauns can be found in stories from ancient Rome.

# Characters: Ordinary or Special?

Characters in fantasy stories are in for a great adventure. They need to be ready for anything. Sometimes the main character is an ordinary person. They may find hidden strengths or powers.

In *The Lion, the Witch and the Wardrobe*, Lucy is an ordinary girl. She accidentally finds the gateway to Narnia. Once in this magic world, Lucy changes. She is a hero who helps defeat the White Witch. She also saves the lion, Aslan.

Some characters in fantasy stories have special powers. The White Witch has great power. She has kept Narnia in an endless winter. She also has helpers who have their own powers. Wolves, dwarves, giants, and ogres are her servants.

Sometimes characters only find their special powers when they are put to a test. It is important to make things difficult for them. Authors put obstacles and problems in their way. Lucy has found a strange world. Can she get back to the wardrobe? Will the gateway still be there?

# World Building: What Are the Rules?

 A fantasy world has to be believable or readers will be pulled out of the story. New worlds need rules as to how people live, work, and act.

Here are some questions you should ask when creating the rules for a new world:

- How is this world arranged? Are there different classes of people, such as wealthy and poor?

- Is there one leader? Is the leader good or evil?

- How does someone become leader? Are they born into it, or do they have to earn the title in some way?

- What jobs do people do, and how do they train for them?

- Where do the characters live? What do they eat?

- How do they get around?

Even if it doesn't make it into the story, an author knows the history of their world. This helps them make decisions about how people will react when an important event happens. It also helps to understand why the events in the story are happening at this point in the world's history. For example, are people facing starvation because there was a drought? Is the land on the brink of war because a leader has died and there is a fight for his spot?

**What do we know about Narnia from the text starting on page 6?**

- Lucy meets Mr Tumnus, the faun. We know that there are at least some mythical creatures living here.

- Mr Tumnus mentions that he has never seen a "Daughter of Eve" before. We know that no humans live here.

- He mentions that it has been winter for a long time. So we know this world has seasons, but is somehow stuck in winter.

- Mr Tumnus also invites Lucy for tea. We know that the creatures in Narnia eat food similar to ours.

Sometimes it is helpful to draw a map of a new world. Seeing it laid out on paper helps us to remember all the things our world needs and where everything is.

# Dialogue: Strange Words

**Some characters speak directly to each other in a text. This is called dialogue. The words that are spoken are surrounded by quotation marks.**

In fantasy stories, characters might speak differently. They might use different phrases for things. Make sure you don't use the phrase, "As busy as a bee" if there are no bees in that world.

How do people speak in this world? Do they speak formally or informally? Can they **pronounce** the same sounds we do?

Mr Tumnus refers to Lucy's spare room as the "land of Spare Oom" and the wardrobe as "city of War Drobe" to show that he has never heard of these things before.

Mr Tumnus calls Lucy a "Daughter of Eve" instead of a girl because he has never seen a human before.

**A robot would speak with funny pauses. You could show this with periods in his dialogue:**

**I. Am. Roboslave. Number. Five. Surrender. Your. Weapons.**

**A medieval knight would speak using Old English phrases:**

*"My good sir. Would thou give me this fair maid's hand in marriage?"*

**Think about how your character will speak. What new words or phrases might they use?**

# Theme: What Is It About?

The theme of a story is the main idea. Fantasy stories are often about a character on a quest. There they meet other characters and face challenges. Themes can be courage, friendship, and honor.

Friendship and loyalty are two themes in *The Lion, the Witch and the Wardrobe*. Lucy and Mr Tumnus are true friends. He refuses to turn her in to the evil White Witch. She also shows great loyalty to him. She does all she can to save him.

Forgiveness is another big theme in this story. Peter, Susan, and Lucy forgive their brother Edmund. They do this right away when he apologizes for siding with the White Witch. Forgiveness is the way relationships heal. Do you think you could have forgiven your brother or sister so quickly?

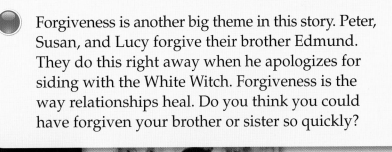

# Creative Response to the Fantasy Story

- Imagine you have just walked through the wardrobe Lucy walked through. You have met either a unicorn, a troll, or a pixie. They have invited you back to their home for tea. Describe their home and what they served you to eat and drink.

- Fantasy stories let the author imagine new creatures. Write a description of a creature you would like to see in a fantasy story. Think about how it will move, eat, and speak.

- Many fantasy characters have a hidden superpower. Superman was fast, strong, and could fly. But kryptonite rendered him powerless. Create a male or female character and give them a superpower. Then think of a way a villain could destroy that power.

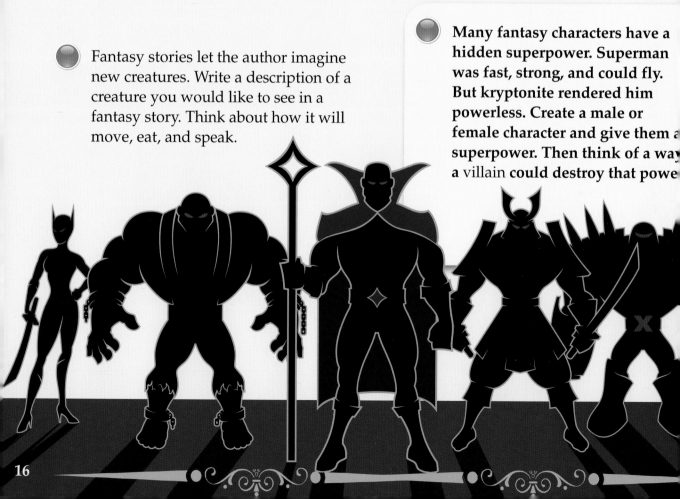

# Peter Pan

The story of *Peter Pan* was written by James Barrie. Peter's adventures were first presented as a play. Later, they were written as a novel.

Peter is the boy who can fly and never grows up. He lives in Neverland and is the leader of his gang, the Lost Boys. Captain Hook is Peter's enemy. Peter cut Hook's hand off in a **duel**. The hand was eaten by a crocodile. The crocodile is hunting Hook because he'd like to eat the rest of him.

On one of Peter's nighttime visits, he meets Wendy, John, and Michael Darling. He uses fairy dust to teach them to fly. They follow him to Neverland.

## Chapter 3

*"It's all right," John announced, emerging from his hiding-place. "I say, Peter, can you really fly?"*

*Instead of troubling to answer him Peter flew around the room, taking the mantelpiece on the way.*

*"How topping!" said John and Michael.*

*"How sweet!" cried Wendy.*

*"Yes, I'm sweet, oh, I am sweet!" said Peter, forgetting his manners again.*

*It looked delightfully easy, and they tried it first from the floor and then from the beds, but they always went down instead of up.*

*"I say, how do you do it?" asked John, rubbing his knee. He was quite a practical boy.*

*"You just think lovely wonderful thoughts," Peter explained, "and they lift you up in the air."*

*He showed them again.*

"You're so nippy at it," John said, "couldn't you do it very slowly once?"

Peter did it both slowly and quickly. "I've got it now, Wendy!" cried John, but soon he found he had not. Not one of them could fly an inch, though even Michael was in words of two syllables, and Peter did not know A from Z.

Of course Peter had been trifling with them, for no one can fly unless the fairy dust has been blown on him. Fortunately, as we have mentioned, one of his hands was messy with it, and he blew some on each of them, with the most superb results.

"Now just wiggle your shoulders this way," he said, "and let go."

They were all on their beds, and gallant Michael let go first. He did not quite mean to let go, but he did it, and immediately he was borne across the room.

"I flewed!" he screamed while still in mid-air.

John let go and met Wendy near the bathroom.

"Oh, lovely!"

"Oh, ripping!"

"Look at me!"

"Look at me!"

"Look at me!"

They were not nearly so elegant as Peter, they could not help kicking a little, but their heads were bobbing against the ceiling, and there is almost nothing so delicious as that. Peter gave Wendy a hand at first, but had to desist, Tink was so indignant.

Up and down they went, and round and round. Heavenly was Wendy's word.

"I say," cried John, "why shouldn't we all go out?"

Of course it was to this that Peter had been luring them.

Michael was ready: he wanted to see how long it took him to do a billion miles. But Wendy hesitated.

"Mermaids!" said Peter again.

"Oo!"

"And there are pirates."

"Pirates," cried John, seizing his Sunday hat, "let us go at once."

*It was just at this moment that Mr. and Mrs. Darling hurried with Nana out of 27. They ran into the middle of the street to look up at the nursery window; and, yes, it was still shut, but the room was ablaze with light, and most heart-gripping sight of all, they could see in shadow on the curtain three little figures in night attire circling round and round, not on the floor but in the air.*

*Not three figures, four!*

*In a tremble they opened the street door. Mr. Darling would have rushed upstairs, but Mrs. Darling signed him to go softly. She even tried to make her heart go softly.*

*Will they reach the nursery in time? If so, how delightful for them, and we shall all breathe a sigh of relief, but there will be no story. On the other hand, if they are not in time, I solemnly promise that it will all come right in the end.*

*They would have reached the nursery in time had it not been that the little stars were watching them. Once again the stars blew the window open, and that smallest star of all called out:*

*"Cave, Peter!"*

*Then Peter knew that there was not a moment to lose. "Come," he cried imperiously, and soared out at once into the night, followed by John and Michael and Wendy.*

*Mr. and Mrs. Darling and Nana rushed into the nursery too late. The birds were flown.*

# Character Flaws

People in real life have good **traits** and bad traits. Characters in fantasy stories should also have strengths and weaknesses. Give your characters some **flaws** so the reader can relate to them. Don't let them be all good or all bad.

In *Peter Pan*, the characters have flaws:

## Peter Pan

In the sample text, Peter was forgetting his manners again." This shows us that, from time to time, Peter is rude and inconsiderate.

## Tinkerbell

We read that "Peter gave Wendy a hand at first, but had to desist, Tink was so indignant." We can see that Tinkerbell is a good friend to Peter. She can also be jealous.

It is a good idea to make your characters afraid, worried, or bothered by something.

In *Peter Pan*, Captain Hook is fierce, but is also afraid of the crocodile hunting him.

# Plot: Making Things Happen

 The plot is the main events of the story. We can picture the plot as a graph.

Introduction → Inciting Incident → Rising Action → Climax → Resolution

A story starts with an **introduction**. This is where we meet the main characters and learn about the setting.

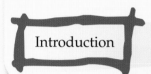 Peter Pan is a boy who can fly. He is listening to Mrs. Darling tell bedtime stories to her children. They are in their home in London.

The **inciting incident** is the event that starts the adventure.

Peter loses his shadow. Wendy reattaches it. He teaches her and her brothers to fly. They leave for Neverland.

The **rising action** is the section where the main character faces a series of problems and obstacles.

- Captain Hook plots his revenge on Peter.
- Wendy acts as mother to the Lost Boys.
- Peter helps the Never Bird.
- Peter rescues Tiger Lily.
- Pirates attack. Wendy and the Lost Boys are taken prisoner.

The **climax** of the story is the most exciting part. This is when the main character is tested and faces the biggest challenge.

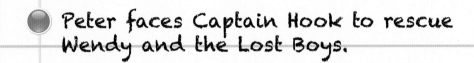 Peter faces Captain Hook to rescue Wendy and the Lost Boys.

The **resolution** is the end of the story when all the loose ends are tied up.

- Wendy and her brothers return home to London.
- The Darlings take in the Lost Boys.
- Peter Pan returns to Neverland.

When working out the plot of a story, it helps to draw a plot graph. It may help to fill in each of the sections. That way you can make sure that you have an interesting and satisfying story.

# Point of View: Who Is Telling This Story

The point of view is the way the author lets the reader know who is telling the story.

Sometimes the main character narrates the story. This is called first person **point of view. The author uses the words "I" and "we".**

 "I hoped the trip would be okay. At least, I hoped that for once I wouldn't get in trouble."—*The Lightning Thief*, **Rick Riordan**

**Sometimes the narrator talks directly to the reader. This is** second person **point of view. Sometimes they use the pronoun "you," but not always.**

 "On the other hand, if they are not in time, I solemnly promise that it will all come right in the end."—*Peter Pan*, **James Barrie**

Third person **point of view is the most common. It feels as though the narrator is watching the events along with the reader. The author uses "he", "she", "it", "they", or proper names to talk about the characters.**

 "As she stood looking at it, wondering why there was a lamp-post in the middle of a wood and wondering what to do next, she heard a pitter patter of feet coming towards her."—*The Lion, the Witch and the Wardrobe*, **C. S. Lewis**

**Which point of view makes you feel more a part of the story? How else are the two stories different? In what ways are they the same? Make a chart to compare them. Then write a compare-and-contrast essay.**

# Dialogue: Watch What You Say

When writing dialogue, it is important to make it sound realistic. It is sometimes useful to spend time listening to people around you speak. Some authors even write down bits of speech that they hear.

Children speak differently than adults. They often have more **emotion** in their speech. Sometimes they make grammar mistakes, too. We can see both of these elements in *Peter Pan*.

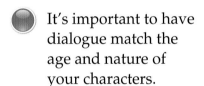 It's important to have dialogue match the age and nature of your characters.

 A small grammar mistake fits Michael's age:

"I flewed!"

 Lots of emotion and excitement:

"How topping!" said John and Michael.

"How sweet!" cried Wendy.

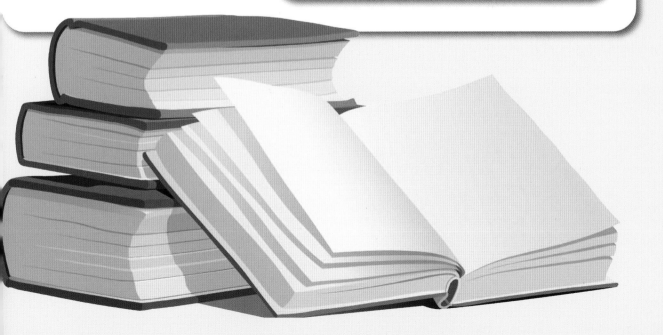

# Creative Response to the Fantasy Story

This story is told from the point of view of a narrator. Choose a character mentioned in the sample (Peter, Wendy, John, Michael, Tinkerbell, Mr. or Mrs. Darling, Nana). Retell the flying scene from this new point of view.

In Peter Pan's world, the rule is that you need fairy dust to fly. Think of a different way that flying could be possible. Write the scene using this new way.

Peter takes Wendy, Michael, and John to Neverland. It is an island with lagoons and forests. Write a description of your own fantasy island. Add different landscapes and homes for creatures. That way, your characters will face dangers and have many adventures there.

# Writing a Fantasy Story

## 1

### Prewriting
### Build Your World

With a fantasy story, it is important to know your world. Think about where you want your story to take place. Is it a world like ours, but with different creatures? Is it another world where everyone floats? Do animals talk? Do trees walk?

*Sample Chart:*
*World's Name: Lupinia*
*Rules:*

- *Lupinia is an island covered with forests and streams.*
- *Pixies live in the flowers.*
- *Trolls live in caves and under rocks along the riverbanks.*
- *Trolls can't come out into the sunshine or else they will dry out and die.*
- *Pixies can't fly when their wings get wet.*
- *Trolls want to eat the pixies.*
- *Pixies have magic powers in their pixie dust.*
- *Trolls can cast curses if they hold a pixie in their hand.*

## 2

### Choose Your Fantasy Elements

Now you know where your story is taking place. Next, you need to decide what fantasy elements to use. Will you have creatures such as faeries, trolls, elves, or dragons? Will your characters deal with magic? Will they have supernatural powers?

*Sample:*
*Fantasy elements in Lupinia:*

- *Pixies*
- *Trolls*
- *Magic*
- *Curses*

### Create Your Characters

Think about your main character and what their strengths are. Does your character know their powers? Or are they just an ordinary person to begin with? Add some other characters for your main character to meet. Give each character a few weaknesses as well as strengths. This will help to make them realistic.

Sample
Main Character: Pixie: Pamela

Strengths: great at flying,
          can outfly any
          other pixie
          brave
          sense of humor

Weaknesses: too curious
            bit of a daredevil

### Plot

Plan the events of your fantasy story. Use a plot graph to help keep all the plot points organized. Introduce your characters and setting. Explain why the events in your story are happening at that point in time. Then think about your inciting incident— what will happen to start the events of your story? What will the climax be? Decide what will lead up to the climax. Put them in as your rising action. Tie up all the plot points in the resolution.

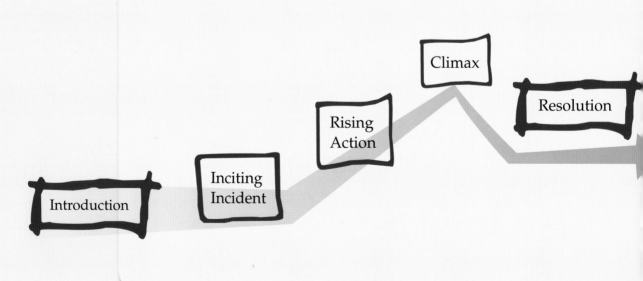

### First Draft

Using your plot graph to keep organized, write out your story. Remember to add dialogue and make it match the age and personality of your characters. Don't worry about it not being perfect—first get the story down. Fixing the plot, characters, and dialogue will come later.

### Revise

Revision means going over your writing and making changes. This is the time to make sure your plot makes sense. Check to make sure your character has strengths and weaknesses. Does your main character face problems in the rising action? Does the climax challenge him or her? Have you answered all questions posed in the story?

Sample:

"Watch me! I can do a loop-de-loop!" Pamela called to her friends.

Pamela soared around the limb of the oak tree. Her wings beat so fast they made a humming noise. She swooped down close to the river. There, in the shade of the river bank, sat a troll.

Bet you can't come close enough to see yourself in the water, the troll said.

He hoped the pixie would forget the danger. She would make a nice snack.

Pamela knew it was dangerous to fly near the water.

Sample:
"Watch me! I can do a loop-de-loop!" Pamela called to her friends.

Pamela soared around the limb of the oak tree. She felt light and free. Her wings beat so fast they made a humming noise. She swooped down close to the river. There, in the shade of the river bank, sat a troll.

Bet you can't come close enough to see yourself in the water, the troll said.

He hoped the pixie would forget the danger. If she came close enough, he could grab her. She would make a nice snack.

Pamela knew it was dangerous to fly near the water, but she wanted to show off.

## Proofread

This is the time to fix mistakes. Check your spelling, grammar, and punctuation.

- Use a dictionary or a spellchecker to make sure all words are spelled correctly. Watch out for homophones. Those are words that sound the same, but are spelled differently. Example: their, they're, and there.

- Do all proper nouns begin with a capital letter?

- Check that dialogue has quotation marks around it.

### Sample:

"Watch me! I can do a loop-de-loop!" Pamela called to her friends.

Pamela soared around the limb of the oak tree. She felt light and free. Her wings beat so fast they made a humming noise. She swooped down close to the river. There, in the shade of the riverbank, sat a troll.

"Bet you can't come close enough to see yourself in the water," the troll said.

He hoped the pixie would forget the danger. If she came close enough, he could grab her. She would make a nice snack.

Pamela knew it was dangerous to fly near the water, but she wanted to show off.

## Final Draft

You have made all your corrections. It is time to write or print out a clean, error-free copy.

# Glossary

**Please note: Some bold-faced words are defined in the text**

| | |
|---|---|
| **drought** | Having no rain for a long time |
| **duel** | A contest between two people to settle a matter of honor |
| **elements** | Parts of something |
| **emotion** | Feelings |
| **flaws** | Defects or imperfections |
| **landscapes** | Features of an area or land |
| **mythical** | Imaginary things found in myths or folktales |
| **obstacles** | Things that block the way |
| **pronounce** | Make the sound of |
| **quest** | A long trip in search of something |
| **supernatural** | Cannot be explained by science |
| **traits** | Parts of a character's personality |
| **villain** | A bad character |
| **wardrobe** | A tall cabinet where clothes are hung |

# Index

# Further Resources

**Books:**

*Activities for Writing Fantasy Stories* by Hilary Braund and Deborah Gibbon. Scholastic (2002)
*Peter Pan* by J. M. Barrie. Sterling (2008)
*The Chronicles of Narnia* by C. S. Lewis. HarperCollins (2011)
*Write Your Own Fantasy: Create Your Own Spellbinding Stories and Enchanting Tales* by Pie Corbett. Pavilion Children's (2013)
*Write Your Own Fantasy Story* by Tish Farrell. Compass Point Books (2008)
*Writing Magic: Creating Stories that Fly* by Gail Carson Levine. HarperCollins (2014)

**Websites:**

A great list of fantasy books for kids:
www.commonsensemedia.org/lists/fantasy-books-for-kids

Great fantasy story starters:
www.scholastic.com/teachers/story-starters/fantasy-writing-prompts/